ANNE FINCH
COUNTESS OF WINCHILSEA

Also by Denys Thompson

The Uses of Poetry (CUP)
Change and Tradition in Rural England (CUP)

Anne Finch
COUNTESS OF WINCHILSEA

Selected Poems

*Edited with an Introduction
and Notes by*
DENYS THOMPSON

Fyfield Books

To my wife

First published in Great Britain 1987 by
Carcanet Press Limited
208-212 Corn Exchange Buildings
Manchester M4 3BQ

and 198 Sixth Avenue, New York
NY 10013

Copyright © 1987 Denys Thompson
Selection, Introduction, Notes

British Library Cataloguing in Publication Data

Winchilsea, Anne Finch, *Countess of*
  Selected poems.
  I. Title   II. Thompson, Denys
  821'.5   PR3765.W57

  ISBN 0-85635-624-7

The publisher acknowledges financial assistance
from the Arts Council of Great Britain

Typeset in 10pt Palatino by Bryan Williamson, Manchester
Printed in England by SRP Ltd, Exeter

Contents

Introduction

ANNE FINCH was born in April 1661, the second daughter of Sir William Kingsmill – a Hampshire family. Her father died a few months after she was born, and her mother five or six years later. Nothing else is known of her life till she was twenty-one, when she was appointed a maid of honour to Mary of Modena, wife of the Duke of York who became James II. She seems to have been happy in the loyalties and conventional piety of her service, in which she enjoyed the friendship of Anne Killigrew, another woman of literary interests. When Mary died in 1718, Anne Finch wrote, in 'On the Death of the Queen':

> Recalled be days when ebon locks o'erspread
> My youthful neck, my cheeks a bashful red;
> When early joys my glowing bosom warmed;
> When trifles pleased and every pleasure charmed;
> Then eager from the rural seat I came
> Of long traced ancestors of worthy name
> To seek the court, of many woes the source,
> Completed by this last, this sad divorce
> From her to whom myself I had resigned:
> The sovereign mistress of my vanquished mind.

In May 1684 she married Col. Heneage Finch, Captain of Halberdiers, a member of the royal household, and later M.P. for Hythe. This was after a persistent courtship, for she records that his 'constant passion found the art / To win a stubborn and ungrateful heart.' He was then twenty-seven and she twenty-three, though in the register she described herself as a spinster 'aged about eighteen years'. The marriage was childless and happy, as his diary and several of her poems bear witness; in her words Heneage was 'the crown and blessing of my life, / The much loved husband of a happy wife.' Her unacted tragedy *Aristomenes* was intended for reading to him, as the Prologue tells us, 'by a good winter's fire'. They lived peacefully at Westminster

7

till 1688, when James and his queen fled the country, and the Finchs, guilty by association with a tyrannical sovereign, fell into poverty and disgrace. In 1690 Heneage attempted to join James on the Continent, but was captured at Hythe; later in the same year he was discharged. The Finchs were then invited by Heneage's nephew, the young Earl of Winchilsea, to live on his estate at Eastwell, in Kent. Life here seems to have suited them both; she preferred country to town, and his scholarly bent found scope in antiquarian pursuits. She suffered however from constitutional depression, and for her health's sake made several visits to Tunbridge Wells and other resorts.

In 1712 Heneage's nephew died, and the uncle succeeded to the peerage; they then returned to London to live at Cleveland Row. Here her confidence increased as she became known to Pope, Swift and other literary figures. She exchanged compliments in verse with Pope, and Purcell set one of her songs to music. Nicholas Rowe in a *New Miscellany of Original Poems* introduced four of her poems with a eulogistic 'Epistle to Flavia'. Now, after following the customary practice of circulating her poems in manuscript, she turned to publication. 'The Spleen' had already appeared separately, and in 1713 a collected edition was published: *Miscellany Poems, written by a lady*. In 1717 Pope paid her the compliment of including eight of her pieces in his own miscellany of *Poems on Several Occasions*. Anne Finch had a serious illness in 1715, and died in April 1720.

Though 'The Spleen' was fairly popular in her lifetime, the reputation of Anne Finch languished after her death for a hundred years. Then, in his middle years, Wordsworth chose sixteen of her titles for an album presented to Lady Mary Lowther at Christmas 1819, introducing the collection with a dedicatory sonnet of his own:

> Lady! I rifled a Parnassian Cave
> (But seldom trod) of mildly gleaming ore;
> And culled, from sundry beds, a lucid store
> Of genuine crystals . . .

And in a later letter to his friend Alexander Dyce he wrote:

> Her style in rhyme is often admirable, chaste, tender, and
> vigorous; and entirely free from sparkle, antithesis, and that
> over-culture which reminds one by its broad glare, its stiff-
> ness and heaviness, of double daisies of the garden, com-
> pared with their modest and sensitive kindred of the fields.

Leigh Hunt followed Wordsworth in praising Anne Finch, and
so did some lesser figures of the nineteenth century, such as
Edmund Gosse and Edward Dowden. In 1903 Myra Reynolds
published in Chicago a complete edition of all the poems then
known, with a full introduction and notes. This has been the
quarry, not always properly acknowledged, for such selections
as Middleton Murry's in 1928 and H. I'A Fausset's of 1930. Virginia Woolf chose a few poems from Murry's small volume to
express a very partial and personal view of Anne Finch in *A Room
of One's Own*'. . . bursting out in indignation against the position
of women . . . harassed and distracted with hates and grievances
. . . bitterness and resentment . . . her gift is all grown about
with weeds and bound with briars . . .' etc. Not the least echo
of this distorted opinion is audible in the best criticism of her
work that has appeared in recent years, by Reuben A. Brower
and Norman Callan. In America there has recently been a good
deal of interest in Anne Finch as a feminist. So today she is
esteemed but unread; and without a new complete edition to
include all the poems found after 1903 it is difficult to get a full
view of her *oeuvre*.

Wordsworth seems to have regarded Anne Finch as a precursor
of his own romantic poetry. 'A Nocturnal Reverie' in particular
appealed strongly to him, and he cites the poem to illustrate a
point in an essay that he appended to the Preface to the second
edition of the *Lyrical Ballads*:

> It is remarkable that, excepting the nocturnal Reverie of
> Lady Winchilsea, and a passage or two in the 'Windsor
> Forest' of Pope, the poetry of the period intervening between

the publication of the *Paradise Lost* and the *Seasons* does not contain a single new image of external nature; and scarcely presents a familiar one from which it can be inferred that the eye of the Poet had been steadily fixed upon his object, much less that his feelings had urged him to work upon it in the spirit of genuine imagination.

Wordsworth approved because she really had seen and heard and felt what she was writing about. Her eye is steadily fixed on the object, and the writing is clear and descriptive. Lines 28-30 of the 'Reverie', for instance, evidently record an actual experience – the big silent shadow appearing from behind, the nose perhaps nuzzling for an apple, and then the scrunching of teeth in the turf. A second reason for his liking must have been lines 37 to the end of the poem:

> When a sedate content the spirit feels,
> And no fierce light disturbs, whilst it reveals;
> But silent musings urge the mind to seek
> Something, too high for syllables to speak;
> Till the free soul to a composedness charmed,
> Finding the elements of rage disarmed,
> O'er all below a solemn quiet grown,
> Joys in the inferior world, and thinks it like her own:
> In such a night let me abroad remain,
> Till morning breaks, and all's confused again;
> Our cares, our toils, our clamours are renewed,
> Or pleasures, seldom reached, again pursued.

Superficially the lines put one in mind of Wordsworth in 'Lines composed above Tintern Abbey':

> And I have felt
> A presence that disturbs me with the joy
> Of elevated thoughts; a sense sublime
> Of something far more deeply interfused,
> Whose dwelling is the light of setting suns . . .

But in trying to enlist Anne Finch's help in making out a case for his own kind of poetry, Wordsworth was straining ineffectively. She was only developing an idea familiar to the religious poets of the seventeenth century: the picture of Nature on earth so lovely that a soul which knows the beauty of heaven can 'joy in the inferior world and think it like her own'.

Anne Finch's work was directed by the moral bent of the period, for she believed that the function of poetry was

> To elevate the hearts of man
> And lead them to those blissful seats again
> Whence all harmonious sounds and lofty numbers flow.

Accordingly her preference for the country over town had a strong moral implication: 'Oh for my groves, my country walks and bowers, / Trees blast not trees, nor flowers envenom flowers.' However this attitude would have had to be pushed a little further before she could be described as anticipating Wordsworth. Whereas the latter deplored man's out-of-tune alienation from nature, the source of strength and consolation:

> The world is too much with us; late and soon,
> Getting and spending, we lay waste our powers;
> Little we see in Nature that is ours;
> We have given our hearts away, a sordid boon!

Anne Finch saw a nature unconcerned with human affairs, in these lines from 'Upon the death of Sir William Twisden':

> But oh! in vain things void of sense we call,
> In vain implore the murmuring sound
> Of hollow groans from underneath the ground,
> Or court the loud lament of some steep water's fall,
> On things inanimate we would force
> Some share of our divided grief,
> Whilst Nature (unconcerned for our relief)
> Pursues her settled path, her fixt and steady course.

Her most popular poem in her day was 'The Spleen', in which

11

without self-pity she mentions various forms of depression. It may be that the poem is an early reflection of the split – the 'divided grief', between man and nature so deeply felt by Wordsworth; but one cannot be sure. Today the 'spleen' seems an odd subject for poetry, but there were other poems, such as Matthew Green's, on the same subject, and not long before Cowley had planned four volumes of verse on the medicinal qualities of herbs. (In former days some professors of medicine had written their textbooks in verse.) It is an engaging poem, learned and analytical, and the source of lines borrowed by Pope and Shelley. When the latter in *Epipsychidion* described the isle 'beautiful as a wreck of Paradise':

> The light clear element which the island wears
> Is heavy with the scent of lemon-flowers,
> Which floats like mist laden with unseen showers,
> And falls upon the eye-lids like faint sleep;
> And from the moss violets and jonquils peep,
> And dart their arrowy odour through the brain
> Till you might faint with that delicious pain . . .

he was using the lines (33-42) in which Anne Finch, addressing spleen as the dull attendant of sin, contrasted the unclogged soul of man in his first state with its condition after the Fall:

> Now the jonquil o'ercomes the feeble brain;
> We faint beneath the aromatic pain,
> Till some offensive scent thy powers appease,
> And pleasure we resign for short and nauseous ease.

Characteristically Shelley replaces 'aromatic' by 'delicious', and enjoys the fainting that was abhorrent to the earlier writer. Later in the poem (lines 82-88) she describes her preference for writing poetry to the usual feminine occupations of painting and embroidery:

> My hand delights to trace unusual things,
> And deviates from the known and common way;

> Nor will in fading silks compose
> Faintly the inimitable rose,
> Fill up an ill-drawn bird, or paint on glass . . .

Both these passages from 'The Spleen' seem to have been in Pope's mind when, in the *Essay on Man* (I), he warns men not to try to exceed their powers:

> . . . To smart and agonise at every pore,
> Or quick effluvia darting through the brain,
> Die of a rose in aromatic pain?

Wordsworth also, when he ended the dedication to his 'Miscellaneous Sonnets', was a borrower; he hoped that the person addressed 'Wilt smile upon this gift with more than mild content', thus echoing Anne Finch's 'Something less than joy, but more than full content.'

These loans to romantic poets are no indication that she was in any sense their fore-runner. Writing in 1891, Edmund Gosse quoted Matthew Arnold's remark to him that the greatest revelation in Humphry Ward's anthology *The English Poets* had been 'the singular merit of Anne Finch', and went on to argue that she was entirely out of sympathy with the age in which she lived. This was not the case. So far as the subjects and manner of her verse were concerned, she was happy in her time. Written in the seventeenth century, her 'On Affliction' is a poem in the fading metaphysical tradition and reminds one of George Herbert; and her later verse is in the satirical and reflective-moralizing mode of the eighteenth century. One of her well-known poems, for example, 'The Petition for an Absolute Retreat', is wholly characteristic of its age, with the wish

> 'mongst paths so lost and trees so high
> That the world may ne'er invade,
> Through such windings and such shade,
> My unshaken liberty –

and for a life of rural peace on country fare, with 'sensible' clothing,

13

no cosmetics, pleasant useful occupations, and

> A partner suited to my mind,
> Solitary, pleased and kind;
> Who partially may something see
> Preferred to all the world in me;
> > Slighting, by my humble side,
> Fame and splendour, wealth and pride.

All this is in the line of Jonson's 'To Penshurst', Carew's 'To my Friend G.N. from Wrest' and Marvell's 'Appleton House' – poems that could be produced only in a steadily continuing rural order, their mood much influenced by Horace and other Latin poets, whom Cowley liked to translate.

She was not an aggressive feminist or the thwarted creative talent invented by Virginia Woolf. The ground for such views lies in her consistent criticism of stock Restoration attitudes, such as the wilful failure to recognise the possibility of love in marriage; 'They err (she wrote), who say that husbands can't be lovers.' Nor could she tolerate the contemporary image of what a woman should be, in 'The Introduction.' After the vigorous opening she contrasts the lot of women in the past with that of her own period:

> How are we fallen! fallen by mistaken rules,
> And Education's, more than Nature's fools,
> Debarred from all improvements of the mind,
> And to be dull, expected and designed . . .

Her main concern was to be allowed to write in peace – to paint thoughts while others paint their faces, and to take to poetry as some women take to the bottle ('The Apology'). She did not write for a living, and so she was never the target for savage attacks by jealous and apprehensive male writers, as was Aphra Behn.

Her output was not large, and some of it is dull, like her religious paraphrases. A staunch churchwoman and Tory, she was a child of her time in political and religious beliefs, as well as in her style. But when she was moved to write about her love for Heneage, her preference for country life, her devotional moods, and her

14

feelings about contemporary attitudes to women, her level is well above that of the other minor poets of her day, and her work of lasting life and value. There is a most pleasing variety of accomplishment in her small *oeuvre*, and she is deservedly anthologised for such pieces as one of Wordsworth's favourites. The lines below are taken from 'All is Vanity'; they exemplify a style not yet sampled by this introduction:

> Trail all your pikes, dispirit every drum,
> March in a slow procession from afar,
> Ye silent, ye dejected men of war!
> Be still the hautboys, and the flute be dumb!
> Display no more, in vain, the lofty banner,
> For see! where on the bier before ye lies
> The pale, the fallen, th' untimely sacrifice
> To your mistaken shrine, to your false idol honour!

The poems up to and including 'To a Fellow Scribbler' were first published as *Miscellany Poems* in 1713, and were reprinted in the Reynolds edition of 1903. 'The Fall of Caesar' is taken from *Pope's Own Miscellany* (1935). The remainder are to be found in the manuscript, a good fair copy of post-1713 poems, at Wellesley College, Massachusetts. Of the six poems from the ms. included here, 'To the Revd Mr Bedford' does not seem to have been printed, though the other Wellesley poems have appeared in books and periodicals – 'The Agreeable' in a version shortened and retitled by Edward Dowden.

Anne Finch was a poor speller with a lack of feeling, surprising in her period, for the derivations and behaviour of English words; and she observed some conventions that would be a hindrance nowadays. Her spelling has therefore been updated.

Acknowledgements

The editor's grateful thanks are due to the staff of the Cambridge University Library; to Dr W.J. Cameron for the chronology of the poems; to Dr Richard Luckett for the loan of Dr Cameron's thesis; to the National Portrait Gallery for the miniature portrait; to Michael Schmidt of the Carcanet Press; and to the Special Collections Librarian of Wellesley College, Massachusetts, for supplying a microfilm copy of the manuscript in the Margaret Clapp Library, together with permission to use the text of 'To the Revd Mr Bedford' and other poems from the manuscript.

16

Fragment

So here confined, and but to female clay,
Ardelia's soul mistook the rightful way:
Whilst the soft breeze of pleasure's tempting air
Made her believe felicity was there,
And, basking in the warmth of early time,
To vain amusements dedicate her prime;
Ambition next allured her towering eye,
For Paradise, she heard, was placed on high,
Then thought, the Court with all its glorious show
Was sure above the rest, and Paradise below.   10
There placed, too soon the flaming sword appeared,
Removed those powers, whom justly she revered,
Adhered to in their wreck, and in their ruin shared.
Now by the wheel's inevitable round,
With them thrown prostrate to the humble ground,
No more she takes (instructed by that fall)
For fixed, or worth her thought, this rolling ball;
Towards a more certain station she aspires,
Unshaken by revolts, and owns no less desires.
But all in vain are prayers, ecstatic thoughts,   20
Recovered moments, and retracted faults.
Retirement, which the world moroseness calls,
Abandoned pleasures in monastic walls:
These, but at distance, towards that purpose tend,
The lowly means to an exalted end;
Which He must perfect who allots her stay,
And, that accomplished, will direct the way,
Pity her restless cares and weary strife,
And point some issue to escaping life;
Which so dismissed, no pen nor human speech   30
The ineffable recess can ever teach;
The expanse, the light, the harmony, the throng,
The bride's attendance, and the bridal song,
The numerous mansions, and the immortal tree,

17

No eye, unpurged by death, must ever see,
Or waves which through that wondrous city roll.
Rest then content, my too impatient soul!
Observe but here the easy precepts given,
Then wait with cheerful hope till heaven be known in heaven.

The Bird

Kind bird, thy praises I design;
Thy praises, like thy plumes, should shine,
Thy praises should thy life outlive
Could I the fame I wish thee give.
Thou my domestic music art
And dearest trifle of my heart.
Soft in thy notes, and in thy dress
Softer than numbers can express;
Softer than love, softer than light,
When first escaping from the night,   10
When first she rises, unarrayed,
And steals a passage through the shade;
Softer than air, or flying clouds
Which Phoebus' glory thinly shrouds;
Gay as the spring, gay as the flowers
When lightly strewed with pearly showers.
Ne'er to the woods shalt thou return,
Nor thy wild freedom shalt thou mourn,
Thou to my bosom shalt repair
And find a safer shelter there.   20
There shalt thou watch, and should I sleep,
My heart, thy charge, securely keep.
Love, who a stranger is to me,
Must by thy wings be kin to thee;
So painted o'er, so seeming fair,
So soft his first addresses are.

Thy guard he ne'er can pass unseen;
Then surely thou hast often been,
Whilst yet a wanderer in the grove
A false accomplice with this love;   30
In the same shade hast thou not sate
And seen him work some wretch's fate?
Hast thou not sooth'd him in the wrong,
And graced the mischief with a song,
Tuning thy loud conspiring voice
O'er falling lovers to rejoice?
If so, thy wicked faults redeem;
In league with me, no truce with him
Do thou admit, but warn my heart,
And all his sly designs impart,   40
Lest to that breast by craft he get
Which has defied and braved him yet.

The Bargain
A song in dialogue between Bacchus and Cupid

CUPID

Bacchus, to thee that turn'st the brain,
And dost o'er mighty punch-bowls reign,
Enthroned upon thy lusty barrel,
I drink to drown the ancient quarrel,
And mortals shall no more dispute
Which of us two is absolute.

BACCHUS

I pledge thee, Archer, nor disdain
To own thou over hearts dost reign,
But tears thou drink'st, drawn from low courage,

And cooled with sighs instead of borage;
Were that error once amended
All might in Champagne be ended.

CUPID

I am content, so we may join
To mix my waters with thy wine;
Then henceforth, farewell all defying,
And thus we'll still be found complying:
He that's in love shall fly to thee,
And he that's drunk shall reel to me.

A Letter to Daphnis

This to the crown and blessing of my life,
The much loved husband of a happy wife;
To him whose constant passion found the art
To win a stubborn and ungrateful heart,
And to the world by tenderest proof discovers
They err, who say that husbands can't be lovers.
With such return of passion as is due,
Daphnis I love, Daphnis my thoughts pursue;
Daphnis, my hopes and joys are bounded all in you.
Even I, for Daphnis' and my promise' sake,
What I in women censure, undertake.
But this from love, not vanity proceeds;
You know who writes, and I who 'tis that reads.
Judge not my passion by my want of skill:
Many love well, though they express it ill;
And I your censure could with pleasure bear,
Would you but soon return, and speak it here.
   April 2nd, 1685

The Tree

Fair tree! for thy delightful shade
'Tis just that some return be made;
Sure some return is due from me
To thy cool shadows, and to thee.
When thou to birds dost shelter give,
Thou music dost from them receive;
If travellers beneath thee stay
Till storms have washed themselves away,
That time in praising thee they spend
And thy protecting power commend.   10
The shepherd here, from scorching freed,
Tunes to thy dancing leaves his reed;
Whilst his loved nymph, in thanks, bestows
Her flow'ry chaplets on thy boughs.
Shall I then only silent be,
And no return be made by me?
No; let this wish upon thee wait,
And still to flourish be thy fate.
To future ages may'st thou stand
Untouched by the rash workman's hand,   20
Till that large stock of sap is spent,
Which gives thy summer's ornament;
Till the fierce winds, that vainly strive
To shock thy greatness whilst alive,
Shall on thy lifeless hour attend,
Prevent the axe, and grace thy end,
Their scattered strength together call
And to the clouds proclaim thy fall;
Who then their evening dews may spare
When thou no longer art their care,   30
But shalt, like ancient heroes, burn,
And some bright hearth be made thy urn.

Clarinda's Indifference at Parting
with her Beauty

Now, age came on, and all the dismal train
That fright the vicious and afflict the vain.
Departing beauty now Clarinda spies,
Pale in her cheeks and dying in her eyes;
That youthful air that wanders o'er the face,
That undescribed, that unresisted grace,
Those morning beams that strongly warm and shine,
Which men that feel and see can ne'er define,
Now, on the wings of restless time, were fled,
And evening shades began to rise and spread;   10
When, thus resolved, and ready soon to part,
Slighting the short reprieves of proffered art,
She spake —
"And what, vain beauty, didst thou e'er achieve,
When at thy height, that I thy fall should grieve?
When didst thou e'er successfully pursue?
When didst thou e'er th' appointed foe subdue?
'Tis vain of numbers, or of strength to boast,
In an undisciplined, unguided host,
And love, that did thy mighty hopes deride,   20
Would pay no sacrifice, but to thy pride.
When didst thou e'er a pleasing rule obtain?
A glorious empire's but a glorious pain.
Thou art, indeed, but vanity's chief source;
But foil to wit, to want of wit a curse:
For often by thy gaudy sign's descried
A fool, which unobserved, had been untried;
And when thou dost such empty things adorn,
'Tis but to make them more the public scorn.
I know thee well, but weak thy reign would be   30
Did none adore or praise thee more than me.
I see, indeed, thy certain ruin near,

But can't afford one parting sigh or tear,
Nor rail at time, nor quarrel with my glass,
But unconcerned, can let thy glories pass."

To Mr F., now Earl of Winchilsea

who, going abroad, had desired Ardelia to write some verses
upon whatever subject she thought fit, against his return in
the evening

No sooner, Flavio, was you gone,
But, your injunction thought upon,
  Ardelia took the pen;
Designing to perform the task
Her Flavio did so kindly ask,
  Ere he returned agen.

Into Parnassus straight she sent,
And bid the messenger that went
  Unto the Muses' court
Assure them she their aid did need,
And begged they'd use their utmost speed,
  Because the time was short.

The hasty summons was allowed;
And, being well bred, they rose and bowed,
  And said they'd post away;
That well they did Ardelia know,
And that no female's voice below
  They sooner would obey:

That many of the rhyming train,
On like occasions, sought in vain
   Their industry to excite;
But for Ardelia all they'd leave;
(Thus flattering can the Muse deceive
   And wheedle us to write)

But, since there was such haste required,
To know the subject 'twas desired
   On which they must infuse;
That they might temper words and rules,
And with their counsel carry tools,
   As country doctors use.

Wherefore, to cut off all delays,
'Twas soon replied, A husband's praise,
   Though in these looser times,
Ardelia gladly would rehearse –
A husband's, who indulged her verse,
   And now required her rhymes.

A husband! echoed all around;
And to Parnassus sure that sound
   Had never yet been sent;
Amazement in each face was read.
In haste the affrighted sisters fled,
   And unto council went.

Erato cried, Since Grizel's days,
Since Troy Town pleased, and Chevy Chase,
   No such design was known;
And 'twas their business to take care
It reached not to the public ear,
   Or got about the town:

Nor came where evening beaux were met
O'er billet doux and chocolate, 50
    Lest it destroyed the house;
For in that place who could dispense
(That wore his clothes with common sense)
    With mention of a spouse?

'Twas put unto the vote at last,
And in the negative it past,
    None to her aid should move;
Yet since Ardelia was a friend,
Excuses 'twas agreed to send,
    Which plausible might prove: 60

That Pegasus of late had been
So often rid through thick and thin
    With neither fear nor wit;
In panegyric been so spurred,
He could not from the stall be stirred,
    Nor would endure the bit.

Melpomene had given a bond
By the new house alone to stand
    And write of war and strife;
Thalia, she had taken fees 70
And stipends from the patentees
    And durst not for her life.

Urania only liked the choice;
Yet not to thwart the public voice,
    She whispering did impart:
They need no foreign aid invoke,
No help to draw a moving stroke,
    Who dictate from the heart.

Enough! the pleased Ardelia cried;
And slighting every Muse beside,   80
    Consulting now her breast,
Perceived that every tender thought,
Which from abroad she'd vainly sought,
    Did there in silence rest;

And should unmoved that post maintain,
Till in his quick return again,
    Met in some neighbouring grove
Where vice nor vanity appear,
Her Flavio them alone might hear
    In all the sounds of love.   90

For, since the world does so despise
Hymen's endearments and its ties,
    They should mysterious be;
Till we that pleasure too possess,
Which makes *their* fancied happiness,
    Of stolen secrecy.

The Introduction

Did I my lines intend for public view,
How many censures would their faults pursue!
Some would, because such words they do affect,
Cry they're insipid, empty, incorrect.
And many have attained, dull and untaught,
The name of wit, only by finding fault.
True judges might condemn their want of wit;
And all might say, they're by a woman writ.
Alas! a woman that attempts the pen,
Such an intruder on the rights of men,   10
Such a presumptuous creature is esteemed,

The fault can by no virtue be redeemed.
They tell us we mistake our sex and way;
Good breeding, fashion, dancing, dressing, play,
Are the accomplishments we should desire;
To write, or read, or think, or to enquire,
Would cloud our beauty, and exhaust our time,
And interrupt the conquests of our prime;
While the dull manage of a servile house
Is held by some our utmost art and use.   20

    Sure, 'twas not ever thus, nor are we told
Fables, of women that excelled of old;
To whom, by the diffusive hand of heaven,
Some share of wit and poetry was given.
On that glad day, on which the Ark returned,
The holy pledge, for which the land had mourned,
The joyful tribes attend it on the way,
The Levites do the sacred charge convey,
Whilst various instruments before it play;
Here, holy virgins in the concert join,   30
The louder notes to soften and refine,
And with alternate verse complete the hymn divine.

    Lo! the young poet, after God's own heart,
By him inspired and taught the Muses' art,
Returned from conquest a bright chorus meets,
That sing his slain ten thousand in the streets.
In such loud numbers they his acts declare,
Proclaim the wonders of his early war,
That Saul upon the vast applause does frown,
And feel its mighty thunder shake the crown.   40
What can the threatened judgment now prolong?
Half of the kingdom is already gone:
The fairest half, whose judgment guides the rest,
Have David's empire o'er their hearts confessed.

    A woman here leads fainting Israel on,
She fights, she wins, she triumphs with a song,
Devout, majestic, for the subject fit,

27

And far above her arms exalts her wit,
Then to the peaceful, shady palm withdraws,
And rules the rescued nation with her laws.   50
    How are we fallen! fallen by mistaken rules,
And Education's, more than Nature's fools;
Debarred from all improvements of the mind,
And to be dull, expected and designed,
And if some one would soar above the rest,
With warmer fancy, and ambition pressed,
So strong the opposing faction still appears,
The hopes to thrive can ne'er outweigh the fears.
Be cautioned, then, my Muse, and still retired;
Nor be despised, aiming to be admired;   60
Conscious of wants, still with contracted wing,
To some few friends, and to thy sorrows sing.
For groves of laurel thou wert never meant:
Be dark enough thy shades, and be thou there content.

To Death

O King of Terrors, whose unbounded sway
All that have life must certainly obey;
The king, the priest, the prophet, all are thine,
Nor would e'en God (in flesh) thy stroke decline.
My name is on thy roll, and sure I must
Increase thy gloomy kingdom in the dust.
My soul at this no apprehension feels,
But trembles at thy swords, thy racks, thy wheels;
The scorching fevers which distract the sense,
And snatch us raving, unprepared from hence;
At thy contagious darts, that wound the heads
Of weeping friends who wait at dying beds.
Spare these, and let thy time be when it will;

My business is to die, and thine to kill.
Gently thy fatal sceptre on me lay,
And take to thy cold arms, insensibly, thy prey.

To a Friend
In Praise of the Invention of Writing Letters

Blest be the man! his memory at least,
Who found the art thus to unfold his breast,
And taught succeeding times an easy way
Their secret thoughts by letters to convey;
To baffle absence and secure delight
Which, till that time, was limited to sight.
The parting farewell spoke, the last adieu,
The less'ning distance past, then loss of view:
The friend was gone which some kind moments gave,
And absence separated like the grave.   10
The wings of love were tender too, till then
No quill thence pulled was shaped into a pen,
To send in paper sheets, from town to town,
Words smooth as they, and softer than his down.
O'er such he reigned, whom neighbourhood had joined,
And hopt from bough to bough supported by the wind.
When for a wife the youthful patriarch sent,
The camels, jewels, and the steward went,
A wealthy equipage, tho' grave and slow:
But not a line that might the lover show.   20
The rings and bracelets wooed her hands and arms;
But had she known of melting words, the charms
That under secret seals in ambush lie
To catch the soul when drawn into the eye,
The fair Assyrian had not took this guide,
Nor her soft heart in chains of pearl been tied.
Had these conveyances been then in date,

Joseph had known his wretched father's state,
Before a famine, which his life pursues,
Had sent his other sons to tell the news.   30
Oh! might I live to see an art arise,
As this to thoughts indulgent to the eyes,
That the dark powers of distance could subdue
And make me *see* as well as *talk* to you:
That tedious miles, nor tracts of air might prove
Bars to my sight, and shadows to my love!
Yet were it granted, such unbounded things
Are wandering wishes, born on fancy's wings,
They'd stretch themselves beyond this happy case,
And ask an art to help us to embrace.   40

To my Sister Ogle

When, dear Teresa, shall I be
By Heaven again restored to you?
Thus, if once more your face I see,
Thus our lost pleasures we'll renew.

Our yesterday, when kindly past,
Shall teach how this should be enjoyed,
And urge to-morrow's eager haste,
As longing to be thus employed.

Time shall pay back the years and hours
That in our absence posted by;   10
Time shall submit to friendship's powers,
And, as we please, shall rest or fly.

The sun that stood to look on war,
And lengthened out that fatal day,

For kindness more engaging far,
Will longer, sure, his fall delay.

At last, when fate the word shall give,
That we no longer here below
This soft, endearing life shall live,
In triumph we'll together go.   20

New arts to find, new joys to try,
The height of friendship to improve;
'Tis worth our pains, and fears to die,
To learn new mysteries of love.
   December 31, 1688

The Change

Poor river, now thou art almost dry,
What nymph or swain will near thee lie?
Since brought alas! to sad decay,
What flocks or herds will near thee stay?
The swans that sought thee in thy pride
Now on new streams forgetful ride:
And fish that in thy bosom lay
Choose in more prosperous floods to play.
All leave thee, now thy ebb appears,
To waste thy sad remains in tears;   10
Nor will thy mournful murmurs heed.
Fly, wretched stream, with all thy speed;
Amongst these solid rocks thy grief bestow;
For friends like those, alas! thou ne'er didst know.

  And thou, poor sun, that sat'st on high,
But late the pleasure of the sky,
What flower, though by thy influence born,

31

Now clouds prevail, will towards thee turn?
Now darkness sits upon thy brow,
What Persian victory will bow?
What river will thy smiles reflect,
Now that no beams thou canst direct?
By watery vapours overcast,
Who thinks upon thy glories past?
If present light nor heat we get,
Unheeded thou mayst rise and set.
Not all the past can one adorer keep;
Fall, wretched sun, to the more faithful deep.

Nor do thou, lofty structure, boast,
Since undermined by time and frost:
Since thou canst no reception give,
In untrod meadows thou mayst live.
None from his ready road will turn
With thee thy wretched change to mourn.
Not the soft nights, or cheerful days
Thou hast bestowed, can give thee praise.
No lusty tree that near thee grows
(though it beneath thy shelter rose)
Will to thy age a staff become;
Fall, wretched building, to thy tomb.
Thou and thy painted roofs in ruin mixed,
Fall to the earth, for that alone is fixed.

The same, poor man, the same must be
Thy fate, now Fortune frowns on thee.
Her favour everyone pursues,
And losing her, thou all must lose.
No love, sown in thy prosperous days,
Can fruit in this cold season raise:
No benefit, by thee conferred,
Can in this time of storms be heard.
All from thy troubled waters run;

Thy stooping fabric all men shun.
All do thy clouded looks decline,
As if thou ne'er didst on them shine.
O wretched man, to other worlds repair,
For faith and gratitude are only there.

On Affliction

Welcome, whate'er my tender flesh may say,
   Welcome affliction, to my reason, still;
Though hard, and rugged on that rock I lay
   A sure foundation, which if raised with skill,
   Shall compass Babel's aim, and reach th' Almighty's hill.

Welcome the rod, that does adoption show,
   The cup, whose wholesome dregs are given me here;
There is a day behind, if God be true,
   When all these clouds shall pass, and heaven be clear,
   When those whom most they shade, shall shine most glorious
      there.

Affliction is the line, which every saint
   Is measured by, his stature taken right;
So much it shrinks, as they repine or faint,
   But if their faith and courage stand upright,
   By that is made the crown, and the full robe of light.

On Myself

Good Heaven, I thank thee, since it was designed
I should be framed but of the weaker kind,
That yet my soul is rescued from the love
Of all those trifles which their passions move.
Pleasures, and praise, and plenty have with me
But their just value. If allowed they be,
Freely and thankfully as much I taste
As will not reason or religion waste.
If they're denied, I on myself can live
And slight those aids unequal chance does give.
When in the sun, my wings can be displayed,
And in retirement, I can bless the shade.

Ardelia to Melancholy

At last, my old, inveterate foe,
No opposition shalt thou know.
Since I, by struggling, can obtain
Nothing, but increase of pain
I will at last no more do so,
Though I confess I have applied
Sweet mirth, and music, and have tried
A thousand other arts beside,
To drive thee from my darkened breast,
Thou, who hast banished all my rest.   10
But though sometimes a short reprieve they gave,
Unable they, and far too weak, to save;
All arts to quell, did but augment thy force,
As rivers checked, break with a wilder course.

Friendship I to my heart have laid,
Friendship, the applauded sovereign aid,
And thought that charm so strong would prove,
As to compel thee to remove;
And to myself I boasting said,
Now I a conqueror sure shall be,   20
The end of all my conflicts see,
And noble triumph wait on me;
My dusky, sullen foe will sure
Ne'er this united charge endure.
But, leaning on this reed, ev'n whilst I spoke,
It pierced my hand, and into pieces broke.
Still some new object, or new interest came
And loosed the bonds, and quite dissolved the claim.

These failing, I invoked a Muse,
And poetry would often use   30
To guard me from thy tyrant power;
And to oppose thee every hour
New troops of fancies did I choose.
Alas! in vain, for all agree
To yield me captive up to thee,
And heaven alone can set me free.
Thou through my life wilt with me go,
And make the passage sad, and slow.
All that could e'er thy ill-got rule invade,
Their useless arms before thy feet have laid;   40
The fort is thine, now ruined all within,
Whilst by decays without, thy conquest too is seen.

An Invocation to Sleep

How shall I woo thee, gentle rest,
To a sad mind with cares oppressed?
By what soft means shall I invite
Thy powers into my soul to-night?
Yet, gentle sleep, if thou wilt come,
Such darkness shall prepare the room
As thy own palace overspreads
(Thy palace, stored with peaceful beds)
And silence too shall on thee wait,
Deep, as in the Turkish state;   10
Whilst still as death I will be found,
My arms by one another bound;
And my dull lids so closed shall be
As if already sealed by thee.
    Thus I'll dispose the outward part.
Would I could quiet too my heart!
But, in its overburthened stead,
Behold I offer thee my head.
My head I better can command,
And that I bow beneath thy hand.   20
Nor do I think that heretofore
Our first great father gave thee more,
When on a flowery bank he lay
And did thy strictest laws obey;
For, to compose his lovely bride,
He yielded not alone his side,
But, if we judge by the event,
Half of his heart too with it went,
Which, wakened, drew him soon away
To Eve's fair bosom, where it lay,   30
Pleased to admit his rightful claim
And tending still towards whence it came.
    Then, gentle sleep, expect from me
No more than I have proffered thee;

For if thou wilt not hear my prayers
Till I have vanquished all my cares,
Thou'lt stay till kinder death supplies thy place,
The surer friend, though with the harsher face.

A Sigh

Gentlest air, thou breath of lovers,
   Vapours from a secret fire,
Which by thee itself discovers,
   Ere yet daring to aspire.

Softest note of whispered anguish,
   Harmony's refin'dest part,
Striking, whilst thou seem'st to languish,
   Full upon the hearer's heart.

Safest messenger of passion,
   Stealing through a crowd of spies,
Which constrain the outward fashion,
   Close the lips and guard the eyes.

Shapeless sigh! we ne'er can show thee,
   Formed but to assault the ear;
Yet, ere to their cost they know thee,
   Every nymph may read thee here.

An Invitation to Daphnis

To leave his study and usual employments – Mathematics,
Paintings, etc. – and to take the pleasures of the fields with
Ardelia

When such a day blessed the Arcadian plain,
Warm without sun, and shady without rain,
Fanned by an air, that scarcely bent the flowers,
Or waved the woodbines on the summer bowers,
The nymphs disordered beauty could not fear,
Nor ruffling winds uncurled the shepherd's hair,
On the fresh grass they trod their measures light,
And a long evening made, from moon to night.
Come then, my Daphnis, from those cares descend
Which better may the winter season spend.   10
    Come, and the pleasures of the fields survey,
      And through the groves with your Ardelia stray.

Reading the softest poetry refuse,
To view the subject of each rural muse;
Nor let the busy compasses go round,
When faery circles better mark the ground.
Rich colours on the vellum cease to lay,
When every lawn much nobler can display,
When on the dazzling poppy may be seen
A glowing red, exceeding your carmine;   20
And for the blue that o'er the sea is borne,
A brighter rises in our standing corn.
    Come then, my Daphnis, and the fields survey,
      And through the groves with your Ardelia stray.

Come, and let Sanson's World no more engage,
Although he gives a kingdom in a page;
O'er all the universe his lines may go,

38

And not a clime like temperate Britain show.
    Come then, my Daphnis, and her fields survey,
      And through the groves with your Ardelia stray.   30

Nor plead that you're immured and cannot yield,
That mighty bastions keep you from the field;
Think not, though lodged in Mons, or in Namur,
You're from my dangerous attacks secure.
No, Louis shall his falling conquests fear,
When by succeeding couriers he shall hear
Apollo and the Muses are drawn down
To storm each fort and take in every town.
Vauban the Orphean lyre to mind shall call,
That drew the stones to the old Theban wall,   40
And make no doubt, if it against him play,
They, from his works, will fly as fast away,
Which to prevent, he shall to peace persuade,
Of strong confederate syllables afraid.
    Come then, my Daphnis, and the fields survey,
      And through the groves with your Ardelia stray.

Come, and attend, how as we walk along,
Each cheerful bird shall treat us with a song,
Not such as fops compose, where wit, nor art,
Nor plainer nature, ever bear a part;   50
The crystal springs shall murmur as we pass,
But not like courtiers, sinking to disgrace;
Nor shall the louder rivers, in their fall,
Like unpaid sailors, or hoarse pleaders, brawl;
But all shall form a concert to delight,
And all to peace, and all to love invite.
    Come then, my Daphnis, and the fields survey.
And through the groves with your Ardelia stray.

As Baucis and Philemon spent their lives,
Of husbands he, the happiest she of wives,   60

39

When through the painted meads their way they sought,
Harmless in act and unperplexed in thought,
Let us, my Daphnis, rural joy pursue,
And courts and camps not even in fancy view.
    So, let us through the groves, my Daphnis, stray,
    And so, the pleasures of the fields survey.

from All is Vanity

Trail all your pikes, dispirit every drum,
March in a slow procession from afar,
Ye silent, ye dejected men of war!
Be still the hautboys, and the flute be dumb!
Display no more, in vain, the lofty banner;
For see! where on the bier before ye lies
The pale, the fall'n, th' untimely sacrifice
To your mistaken shrine, to your false idol honour!

The Spleen
A Pindaric Poem

What art thou, Spleen, which everything dost ape?
    Thou Proteus to abused mankind,
    Who never yet thy real cause could find
Or fix thee to remain in one continued shape.
    Still varying thy perplexing form
    Now a Dead Sea thou'lt represent,
    A calm of stupid discontent,
Then, dashing on the rocks, with rage into a storm.
    Trembling sometimes thou dost appear
    Dissolved into a panic fear;   10
    Or sleep intruding dost thy shadows spread

And crowd with boding dreams the melancholy head;
    Or when the midnight hour is told
    And drooping lids thou still dost waking hold,
    Thy fond delusions cheat the eyes;
    Before them antic spectres dance,
Unusual fires their pointed heads advance
    And airy phantoms rise.
    Such was the monstrous vision seen
When Brutus (now beneath his cares oppressed   20
And all Rome's fortunes rolling in his breast
    Before Philippi's latest field,
Before his fate did to Octavius yield)
    Was vanquished by the Spleen.

    Falsely, the mortal part we blame
    Of our depressed and ponderous frame,
    Which, till the first degrading Sin
    Let thee its dull attendant in,
    Still with the other did comply,
Nor clogged the active soul, disposed to fly   30
And range the mansions of its native sky.
    Nor whilst in his own heaven he dwelt
    Whilst man his Paradise possessed,
His fertile garden in the fragrant east,
    And all united odours smelt,
    No armed sweets until thy reign
    Could shock the sense, or in the face
    A flushed, unhandsome colour place.
Now the jonquil o'ercomes the feeble brain;
We faint beneath the aromatic pain,   40
Till some offensive scent thy powers appease,
And pleasure we resign for short and nauseous ease.

    In every one thou dost possess
    New are thy motions and thy dress;
    Now in some grove a listening friend

41

Thy false suggestions must attend,
Thy whispered griefs, thy fancied sorrows hear,
Breathed in a sigh and witnessed by a tear;
    Whilst in the light and vulgar crowd
    Thy slaves, more clamorous and loud,   50
By laughters unprovoked thy influence too confess.
In the imperious wife thou Vapours art,
    Which from o'erheated passions rise
    In clouds to the attractive brain
    Until, descending thence again,
    Through the o'ercast and showering eyes,
    Upon her husband's softened heart,
    He the disputed point must yield,
Something resign of the contested field;
Till lordly man, born to imperial sway,   60
Compounds for peace, to make that right away
And woman, armed with spleen, does servilely obey.

    The fool, to imitate the wits,
    Complains of thy pretended fits,
    And dullness, born with him, would lay
    Upon thy accidental sway;
    Because sometimes thou dost presume
    Into the ablest heads to come:
    That often men of thoughts refined,
    Impatient of unequal sense,   70
Such slow returns where they so much dispense,
Retiring from the crowd, are to thy shades inclined.
    O'er me, alas! thou dost too much prevail:
    I feel thy force whilst I against thee rail:
I feel my verse decay, and my cramped numbers fail.
Through thy black jaundice I all objects see
    As dark, as terrible as thee,
My lines decried, and my employment thought
An useless folly or presumptuous fault:
    Whilst in the Muses' paths I stray,   80

Whilst in their groves and by their secret springs
My hand delights to trace unusual things,
And deviates from the known and common way;
    Nor will in fading silks compose
    Faintly the inimitable rose,
Fill up an ill-drawn bird, or paint on glass
The Sovereign's blurred and undistinguished face,
The threatening angel and the speaking ass.

Patron thou art to every gross abuse,
    The sullen husband's feigned excuse   90
When the ill-humour with his wife he spends
And bears recruited wit and spirits to his friends.
    The son of Bacchus pleads thy power
    As to the glass he still repairs,
    Pretends but to remove thy cares,
Snatch from thy shades one gay and smiling hour
And drown thy kingdom in a purple shower.
When the coquette, whom every fool admires,
    Would in variety be fair,
    And changing hastily the scene   100
    From light, impertinent and vain,
Assumes a soft, a melancholy air,
And of her eyes rebates the wandering fires,
The careless posture and the head reclined,
    The thoughtful and composed face,
Proclaiming the withdrawn, the absent mind,
Allows the fop more liberty to gaze,
Who gently for the tender cause inquires.
The cause, indeed, is a defect in sense,
Yet is the spleen alleged and still the dull pretence.   110
    But these are thy fantastic harms,
    The tricks of thy pernicious stage,
    Which do the weaker sort engage;
Worse are the dire effects of thy more powerful charms.
    By thee Religion, all we know

43

That should enlighten here below,
Is veiled in darkness and perplexed.
With anxious doubts and endless scruples vexed
And some restraint implied from each perverted text;
Whilst *Touch not, Taste not* what is freely given 120
Is but thy niggard voice disgracing bounteous heaven.
From speech restrained, by thy deceits abused,
To deserts banished or in cells reclused,
Mistaken votaries to the Powers Divine,
Whilst they a purer sacrifice design,
Do but the spleen obey, and worship at thy shrine.
In vain to chase thee every art we try,
In vain all remedies apply,
In vain the Indian leaf infuse,
Or the parched Eastern berry bruise; 130
Some pass in vain these bounds and nobler liquors use.
Now harmony in vain we bring,
Inspire the flute and touch the string.
From harmony no help is had;
Music but soothes thee, if too sweetly sad,
And if too light, but turns thee gaily mad.
Though the physician's greatest gains,
Although his growing wealth he sees
Daily increased by ladies' fees,
Yet dost thou baffle all his studious pains. 140
Not skilful Lower thy source could find
Or through the well-dissected body trace
The secret, the mysterious ways,
By which thou dost surprise and prey upon the mind.
Though in the search, too deep for human thought,
With unsuccessful toil he wrought,
Till, thinking thee to have catched, himself by thee was caught,
Retained thy prisoner, thy acknowledged slave,
And sunk beneath thy chain to a lamented grave.

Ardelia's Answer to Ephelia

who had invited her to come to town: reflecting on the
coquetterie and detracting humour of the age

Me, dear Ephelia, me in vain you court
With all your powerful influence to resort
To that great town, where Friendship can but have
The few spare hours which meaner pleasures leave.
No! let some shade, or your large palace be
Our place of meeting, love and liberty,
To thoughts and words and all endearments free.
But to those walls excuse my slow repair
Who have no business, or diversion there,
No dazzling beauty to attract the gaze   10
Of wandering crowds to my applauded face;
Nor to my little wit the ill nature joined
To pass a general censure on mankind:
To call the young and unaffected, fools;
Dull, all the grave, that live by moral rules;
To say the soldier brags, who, asked, declares
The nice escapes and dangers of his wars,
The poet's vain that knows his unmatched worth,
And dares maintain what the best Muse brings forth:
Yet this the humour of the age is grown   20
And only conversation of the town.
In satire versed and sharp detraction be,
And you're accomplished for all company.
   When my last visit I to London made
Me to Almeria wretched chance betrayed;
The fair Almeria, in this art so known,
That she discerns all failings but her own.
With a loud welcome and a strict embrace,
Kisses on kisses, in a public place,
She extorts a promise that next day I dine   30
With her who for my sight did hourly pine,

And wonders how so far I can remove
From the beau monde, and the dull country love;
Yet vows, if but an afternoon 'twould cost,
To see me there she could resolve almost
To quit the town and for that time be lost.
   My word I keep; we dine, then rising late,
Take coach which long had waited at the gate;
About the streets a tedious ramble go
To see this monster, or that waxwork show,   40
Or anything that may the time bestow.
When by a church we pass, I ask to stay,
Go in, and my devotions humbly pay
To that great Power whom all the wise obey.
Whilst the gay thing, light as her feathered dress,
Flies round the coach, and does each cushion press,
Through every glass her several graces shows;
This does her face, and that her shape expose
To envying beauties and admiring beaux.
One stops, and as expected all extols,   50
Clings to the door, and on his elbow lolls,
Thrusts in his head, at once to view the fair.
And keeps his curls from discomposing air,
Then thus proceeds:
                    "My wonder it is grown
To find Almeria here, and here alone.
Where are the nymphs that round you used to crowd,
Of your long courted approbation proud,
Learning from you how to erect their hair,
And in perfection all their habit wear,
To place a patch in some peculiar way   60
That may an unmarked smile to sight betray
And the vast genius of the sex display?"
   "Pity me then," she cries, "and learn the fate
That makes me porter to a temple gate.
Ardelia came to town some weeks ago
Who does on books her rural hours bestow

And is so rustic with her clothes and mien,
'Tis with her ungenteel but to be seen
Did not a long acquaintance plead excuse;
Besides, she likes no wit that's now in use,   70
Despises courtly vice, and plainly says
That sense and nature should be found in plays,
And therefore none will e'er be bought to see
But those of Dryden, Etherege and Lee,
And some few authors, old and dull to me.
To her I did engage my coach and day,
And here must wait, while she within does pray.
Ere twelve was struck she calls me from my bed,
Not once observes how well my toilet's spread;
Then drinks the fragrant tea contented up,   80
Without a compliment upon the cup,
Though to the ships for the first choice I steered
Through such a storm as the stout bargemen feared,
Lest that a praise, which I have long engrossed,
Of the best china equipage be lost.
Of fashions now and colours I discoursed,
Detected shops that would expose the worst,
What silks, what lace, what ribans she must have,
And by my own an ample pattern gave.
To which she cold and unconcerned replied,   90
'I deal with one that does all these provide,
Having of other cares enough beside;
And in a cheap, or an ill-chosen gown,
Can value blood that's nobler than my own,
And therefore hope myself not to be weighed
By gold or silver on my garments laid;
Or that my wit or judgment should be read
By an uncommon colour on my head.' "
    "Stupid, and dull," the shrugging zany cries;
When, service ended, me he moving spies,   100
Hastes to conduct me out and in my ear
Drops some vile praise too low for her to hear;

47

Which to avoid more than the begging throng,
I reach the coach, that swiftly rolls along
Lest to Hyde Park we should too late be brought
And lose ere night an hour of finding fault.
Arrived, she cries:
                    "That awkward creature see,
A fortune born, and would a beauty be
Could others but believe as fast as she."
   Round me I look some monster to descry   110
Whose wealthy acres must a title buy,
Support my Lord, and be, since his have failed,
With the high shoulder, on his race entailed;
When to my sight a lovely face appears,
Perfect in everything but growing years.
This I defend, to do my judgment right.
"Can you dispraise a skin so smooth, so white,
That blush which o'er such well-turned cheeks does rise, –
That look of youth, and those enliven'd eyes?"
   She soon replies: 120
                    "That skin which you admire
Is shrunk and sickly, could you view it nigher.
The crimson lining and uncertain light
Reflects that blush, and paints her to the sight.
Trust me, the look which you commend betrays
A want of sense more than the want of days;
And those wild eyes that round the circle stray
Seem as her wits had but mistook their way."
   "As I did mine," I to myself repeat,
"When by this envious side I took my seat."
O for my groves, my country walks and bowers!   130
Trees blast not trees, nor flowers envenom flowers,
As beauty here all beauty's praise devours.
But noble Piso passes.
                    "He's a wit,
As some (she says) would have it, though as yet
No line he in a lady's fan has writ,

Ne'er on their dress, in verse, soft things would say,
Or with loud clamour overpowered a play
And right or wrong prevented the third day;
To read in public places is not known,
Or in his chariot here appears alone; 140
Bestows no hasty praise on all that's new.
When first this coach came out to public view,
Met in a visit, he presents his hand
And takes me out. I make a wilful stand,
Expecting, sure this would applause invite,
And often turned that way to guide his sight;
Till, finding him wrapped in a silent thought,
I asked, if that the painter well had wrought?
Who then replied, 'He has in the fable erred,
Covering Adonis with a monstrous beard; 150
Made Hercules (who by his club is shown)
A gentler fop than any of the town;
Whilst Venus from a bog is rising seen
And eyes asquint are given to beauty's queen.'
I had no patience longer to attend,
And know 'tis want of wit to discommend."
    Must Piso then be judged by such as these? –
Piso who from the Latin Virgil freed,
Who loosed the bands which old Silenus bound,
And made our Albion rocks repeat the mystic sound, 160
Whilst all he sung was present to our eyes,
And as he raised his verse, the poplars seemed to rise?
Scarce could I in my breast my thoughts contain,
Or for this folly hide my just disdain.
When "See," she says, "observe my best of friends!"
And through the window half her length extends,
Exalts her voice that all the ring may hear
How fulsomely she oft repeats "My dear!"
Lets fall some doubtful words that we may know
There still a secret is betwixt them two, 170
And makes a sign, the small white hand to show;

49

When, fate be praised, the coachman slacks the reins,
And o'er my lap no longer now she leans,
But how her choice I like does soon inquire.
   "Can I dislike," I cry, "what all admire?
Discreet and witty, civil and refined
Nor in her person fairer than her mind
Is young Alinda, if report be just;
For half her character my eyes I trust.
What! changed Almeria? on a sudden cold?   180
As if I of your friend some tale had told?"
"No," she replies. "But when I hear her praise,
A secret failing does my pity raise.
Damon she loves, and 'tis my daily care
To keep the passion from the public ear."
   I ask, amazed, if this she has revealed.
"No, but 'tis true," she cries, "though much concealed.
I have observed it long, nor would betray
But to yourself what now with grief I say,
Who this to none but confidents must break,   190
Nor they to others but in whispers speak.
I am her friend and must consult her fame."
More she was saying when fresh objects came
   "Now what's that thing," she cries. "Ardelia! guess."
   "A woman, sure."
                  "Aye, and a poetess!
They say she writes, and 'tis a common jest."
   "Then sure she has publicly the skill professed,"
I soon reply, "or makes that gift her pride,
And all the world but scribblers does deride;
Sets out lampoons where only spite is seen,   200
Not filled with female wit, but female spleen;
Her flourished name does o'er a song expose,
Which through all ranks down to the carman goes;
Or poetry is on her picture found
In which she sits with painted laurel crowned.
If no such flies, no vanity defile

50

The Heliconian balm, the sacred oil,
Why should we from that pleasing art be tied,
Or, like state-prisoners, pen and ink denied?
But see, the Sun his chariot home has driven   210
From the vast shining ring of spacious heaven,
Nor after him celestial beauties stay
But crowd with sparkling wheels the Milky Way.
Shall we not then the great example take
And ours below with equal speed forsake?
When to your favours, adding this one more,
You'll stop, and leave me thankful, at my door."

    "How! Ere you've in the Drawing-room appeared
And all the follies there beheld and heard!
Since you've been absent such intrigues are grown,   220
Such new coquettes and fops are to be shown,
Without their sight you must not leave the town."

    "Excuse me," I reply. "My eyes ne'er feast
Upon a fool, though ne'er so nicely drest.
Nor is it music to my burthened ear
The unripe pratings of our sex to hear;
A noisy girl, who's at fifteen talked more
Than grandmother or mother heretofore
In all the cautious, prudent years they bore."

    "Statesmen there are," she cried, "whom I can show   230
That bear the kingdom's cares on a bent brow;
Who take the weight of politics by grains
And, to the least, know what each skull contains;
Who's to be coached, who talked to, when abroad,
Who but the smile must have, and who the nod;
And when this is the utmost of their skill,
'Tis not much wonder if affairs go ill.
Then for the Churchmen –"

                               "Hold, my lodging's here!"
Nor can I longer a reproof forbear
When sacred things nor persons she would spare.   240

    We parted thus, the night in peace I spent,

51

And the next day with haste and pleasure went
To the best seat of famed and fertile Kent.
Where let me live from all detraction free
Till thus the world is criticized by me;
Till friend and foe I treat with such despite,
May I no scorn, the worst of ills, excite!

Friendship
between Ardelia and Ephelia

Eph. What Friendship is, Ardelia, show.
Ard. 'Tis to love as I love you.
Eph. This account, so short (though kind)
      Suits not my enquiring mind.
      Therefore farther now repeat:
      What is Friendship when complete?
Ard. 'Tis to share all joy and grief;
      'Tis to lend all due relief
      From the tongue, the heart, the hand,
      'Tis to mortgage house and land;
      For a friend be sold a slave;
      'Tis to die upon a grave
      If a friend do therein lie.
Eph. This indeed, though carried high;
      This, though more than e'er was done
      Underneath the rolling sun,
      This has all been said before.
      Can Ardelia say no more?
Ard. Words indeed no more can show:
      But 'tis to love as I love you.

The Petition for an Absolute Retreat

inscribed to the Right Honble Catherine Countess of Thanet,
mentioned in the Poem under the name of Arminda

Give me, O indulgent fate!
Give me yet before I die
A sweet, yet absolute retreat,
'Mongst paths so lost and trees so high
That the world may ne'er invade
Through such windings and such shade
My unshaken liberty.

No intruders thither come
Who visit but to be from home!
None who their vain moments pass   10
Only studious of their glass;
News, that charm to listening ears,
That false alarm to hopes and fears,
That common theme for every fop,
From the statesman to the shop,
In those coverts ne'er be spread,
Of who's deceased, and who's to wed.
Be no tidings thither brought,
But silent as a midnight thought
Where the world may ne'er invade   20
Be those windings and that shade!
   Courteous Fate! afford me there
A table spread, without my care,
With what the neighbouring fields impart,
Whose cleanliness be all its art.
When of old the calf was dressed
(Though to make an angel's feast)
In the plain unstudied sauce
Nor truffle nor morillia was;
Nor could the mighty patriarchs' board   30

53

One far-fetched ortolan afford.
Courteous Fate! then give me there
Only plain and wholesome fare;
Fruits indeed (would heaven bestow)
All, that did in Eden grow
All but the forbidden Tree
Would be coveted by me;
Grapes with juice so crowded up
As breaking through the native cup;
Figs yet growing candied o'er 40
By the sun's attracting power;
Cherries, with the downy peach,
All within my easy reach;
Whilst creeping near the humble ground
Should the strawberry be found
Springing whereso'er I strayed
Through those windings and that shade.

For my garments: let them be
What may with the time agree;
Warm when Phoebus does retire 50
And is ill-supplied by fire:
But when he renews the year
And verdant all the fields appear.
Beauty every thing resumes,
Birds have dropped their winter plumes,
When the lily full-displayed
Stands in purer white arrayed
Than that vest which heretofore
The luxurious monarch wore,
When from Salem's gates he drove 60
To the soft retreat of love,
Lebanon's all burnished house
And the dear Egyptian spouse.
Clothe me, Fate, though not so gay,
Clothe me light and fresh as May!

In the fountains let me view
All my habit cheap and new
Such as, when sweet zephyrs fly,
With their motions may comply,
Gently waving to express   70
Unaffected carelessness.
No perfumes have there a part
Borrowed from the Chemist's art,
But such as rise from flowery beds
Or the falling jasmine sheds!
'Twas the odour of the field
Esau's rural coat did yield
That inspired his father's prayer
For blessings of the earth and air:
Of gums and powders had it smelt   80
The supplanter, then unfelt,
Easily had been descried
For one that did in tents abide,
For some beauteous handmaid's joy,
And his mother's darling boy.
Let me then no fragrance wear
But what the winds from gardens bear,
In such kind surprising gales
As gathered from Fidentia's vales
All the flowers that in them grew;   90
Which intermixing as they slew
In wreathen garlands dropped agen
On Lucullus and his men;
Who, cheered by the victorious sight,
Trebled numbers put to flight.
    Let me, when I must be fine,
In such natural colours shine;
Wove and painted by the sun;
Whose resplendent rays to shun
When they do too fiercely beat   100
Let me find some close retreat

Where they have no passage made
Through those windings, and that shade.

   Give me there (since Heaven has shown
It was not good to be alone)
A partner suited to my mind,
Solitary, pleased and kind;
Who partially may something see
Preferred to all the world in me;
Slighting, by my humble side,   110
Fame and splendour, wealth and pride.
When but two the earth possessed,
'Twas their happiest days, and best;
They by business, nor by wars,
They by no domestic cares,
From each other e'er were drawn
But in some grove or flowery lawn
Spent the swiftly flying time,
Spent their own and nature's prime,
In love: that only passion given   120
To perfect man, whilst friends with heaven.
Rage, and jealousy, and hate,
Transports of his fallen state,
(When by Satan's wiles betrayed)
Fly those windings, and that shade!

   Thus from crowds and noise removed,
Let each moment be improved,
Every object still produce
Thoughts of pleasure, and of use;
When some river slides away   130
To increase the boundless sea,
Think we then, how Time does haste
To grow Eternity at last;
By the willows, on the banks,
Gathered into social ranks,

Playing with the gentle winds,
Straight the boughs and smooth the rinds,
Moist each fibre, and each top
Wearing a luxurious crop,
Let the time of youth be shown, 140
The time, alas! too soon outgrown;
Whilst a lonely stubborn oak
Which no breezes can provoke,
No less gusts persuade to move
Than those which in a whirlwind drove,
Spoiled the old fraternal feast
And left alive but one poor guest,
Rivelled the distorted trunk,
Sapless limbs all bent and shrunk,
Sadly does the time presage 150
Of our too near approaching age.
When a helpless vine is found
Unsupported on the ground,
Careless all the branches spread,
Subject to each haughty tread,
Bearing neither leaves, nor fruit,
Living only in the root;
Back reflecting let me say
So the sad Ardelia lay
Blasted by a storm of fate 160
Felt through all the British state;
Fallen, neglected, lost, forgot,
Dark oblivion all her lot;
Faded till Arminda's love
(Guided by the powers above)
Warmed anew her drooping heart
And life diffused through every part;
Mixing words of wise discourse
Of such weight and wondrous force
As could all her sorrows charm 170
And transitory ills disarm;

Cheering the delightful day,
When disposed to be more gay,
With wit from an unmeasured store
To woman ne'er allowed before.
What nature, or refining art,
All that fortune could impart,
Heaven did to Arminda send,
Then gave her for Ardelia's friend:
To her cares the cordial drop   180
Which else had overflowed the cup.
So when once the son of Jess
Every anguish did oppress,
Hunted by all kinds of ills,
Like a partridge on the hills;
Trains were laid to catch his life,
Baited with a royal wife,
From his house and country torn,
Made a heathen prince's scorn;
Fate to answer all these harms   190
Threw a friend into his arms.
Friendship still has been designed
The support of human-kind;
The safe delight, the useful bliss,
The next world's happiness, and this.
Give then, O indulgent fate!
Give a friend in that retreat
(Though withdrawn from all the rest)
Still a clue to reach my breast.
Let a friend be still conveyed   200
Through those windings and that shade!

   Where, may I remain secure;
Waste, in humble joys and pure,
A life that can no envy yield;
Want of affluence my shield.
Thus had Crassus been content,

When from Marius' rage he went,
With the seat that fortune gave,
The commodious, ample cave,
Formed in a divided rock,   210
By some mighty earthquake's shock,
Into rooms of every size,
Fair as art could e'er devise,
Leaving, in the marble roof,
('Gainst all storms and tempests proof)
Only passage for the light
To refresh the cheerful sight;
Whilst three sharers in his fate
On the escape with joy dilate,
Beds of moss their bodies bore,   220
Canopied with ivy o'er;
Rising springs that round them played
O'er the native pavement strayed;
When the hour arrived to dine
Various meats and sprightly wine
On some neighbouring cliff they spied,
Every day anew supplied
By a friend's entrusted care.
Had he still continued there,
Made that lonely wondrous cave   230
Both his palace and his grave,
Peace and rest he might have found
(Peace and rest are underground)
Nor have been in that retreat
Famed for a proverbial fate;
In pursuit of wealth been caught
And punished with a golden draught.
    Nor had he, – who crowds could blind,
Whispering with a snowy hind,
Made them think that from above   240
(Like the great impostor's dove)
Tidings to his ears she brought,

Rules by which he marched and fought,
After Spain he had o'er-run,
Cities sacked, and battles won,
Drove Rome's consuls from the field,
Made her darling Pompey yield, –
At a fatal, treacherous feast
Felt a dagger in his breast;
Had he his once pleasing thought   250
Of solitude to practice brought;
Had no wild ambition swayed;
In those islands had he stayed,
Justly called the seats of rest,
Truly fortunate, and blest,
By the ancient poets given
As their best discovered Heaven.

    Let me then, indulgent Fate!
Let me still in my retreat,
From all roving thoughts be freed,   260
Or aims that may contention breed;
Nor be my endeavours led
By goods that perish with the dead!
Fitly might the life of man
Be indeed esteemed a span,
If the present moment were
Of delight his only share;
If no other joys he knew
Than what round about him grew:
But as those who stars would trace   270
From a subterranean face
Through some engine lift their eyes
To the outward, glorious skies;
So the immortal spirit may,
When descended to our clay,
From a rightly governed frame
View the height from whence she came;

To her paradise be caught
And things unutterable taught.
Give me then, in that retreat,   280
Give me, O indulgent Fate!
For all pleasures left behind
Contemplations of the mind.
Let the fair, the gay, the vain
Courtship and applause obtain;
Let the ambitious rule the earth;
Let the giddy fool have mirth;
Give the epicure his dish,
Every one their several wish;
Whilst my transports I employ   290
On that more extensive joy,
When all Heaven shall be surveyed
From those windings, and that shade.

The Apology

'Tis true, I write; and tell me by what rule
I am alone forbid to play the fool,
To follow through the groves a wandering muse
And feigned ideas for my pleasures choose?
Why should it in my pen be held a fault,
Whilst Myra paints her face, to paint a thought?
Whilst Lamia to the manly bumper flies,
And borrowed spirits sparkle in her eyes,
Why should it be in me a thing so vain
To heat with poetry my colder brain?

But I write ill, and therefore should forbear.
Does Flavia cease now at her fortieth year
In every place to let that face be seen
Which all the town rejected at fifteen?

Each woman has her weakness; mine indeed
Is still to write, though hopeless to succeed.
Nor to the men is this so easy found;
Even in most works with which the wits abound
(So weak are all since our first breach with Heaven)
There's less to be applauded than forgiven.

Enquiry after Peace
a Fragment

Peace! where art thou to be found?
Where, in all the spacious round,
May thy footsteps be pursued?
Where may thy calm seats be viewed?
On some mountain dost thou lie,
Serenely near the ambient sky,
Smiling at the clouds below,
Where rough storms and tempests grow?
Or, in some retired plain,
Undisturbed dost thou remain?   10
Where no angry whirlwinds pass,
Where no floods oppress the grass,
High above, or deep below,
Fain I thy retreat would know.
Fain I thee *alone* would find,
Balm to my o'er-wearied mind.
Since what here the world enjoys,
Or our passions most employs,
Peace opposes, or destroys.
Pleasure's a tumultuous thing,   20
Busy still, and still on wing;
Flying swift from place to place,
Darting from each beauteous face,
From each strongly mingled bowl,

Through th' inflamed and restless soul.
Sov'reign pow'r who fondly craves
But himself to pomp enslaves,
Stands the envy of mankind,
Peace in vain attempts to find.
Thirst of wealth no quiet knows,   30
But near the death-bed fiercer grows,
Wounding men with secret stings,
For evils it on others brings.
War who not discreetly shuns,
Thorough life the gauntlet runs:
Swords, and pikes, and waves, and flames,
Each their stroke against him aims.
Love (if such a thing there be)
Is all despair, or ecstasy.
Poetry's the feverish fit,   40
Th' o'erflowing of unbounded wit. . . .

Adam Posed

Could our first father, at his toilsome plough,
Thorns in his path, and labour on his brow,
Clothed only in a rude unpolished skin,
Could he a vain fantastic nymph have seen,
In all her airs, in all her antic graces,
Her various fashions, and more various faces;
How had it posed that skill, which late assigned
Just appellations to each several kind,
A right idea of the sight to frame,
To have guessed from what new element she came,
To have hit the wavering form, or given this thing a name!

Jupiter and the Farmer

When poets gave their god in Crete a birth,
Then Jupiter held traffic with the earth,
And had a farm to let. The fine was high,
For much the treas'ry wanted a supply,
By Danaë's wealthy show'r exhausted quite, and dry.
But Merc'ry, who as steward kept the court,
So racked the rent that all who made resort
Unsatisfied returned, nor could agree
To use the lands, or pay his secret fee:
Till one poor clown (thought subtler than the rest   10
Thro' various projects rolling in his breast)
Consents to take it, if at his desire
All weathers towards his harvest may conspire:
The frost to kill the worm, the brooding snow,
The filling rains may come, and Phoebus glow.
The terms accepted, signed and sealed the lease,
His neighbour's grounds afford their due increase,
The care of heaven; the owner's cares may cease;
Whilst the new tenant, anxious in his mind,
Now asks a shower, now craves a rustling wind   20
To raise what that had lodged, that he the sheaves may bind.
The sun, th' o'er-shadowing clouds, the moistening dews,
He with such contrariety does choose:
So often and so oddly shifts the scene,
Whilst others load, he scarce has what to glean.

O Jupiter! with famine pinched he cries,
No more will I direct th' unerring skies;
No more my substance on a project lay,
No more a sullen doubt I will betray:
Let me but live to reap, do thou appoint the way.   30

Love, Death, and Reputation

Reputation, Love, and Death,
(The last all bones, the first all breath,
The midst composed of restless fire)
From each other would retire;
Through the world resolved to stray,
Every one a several way;
Exercising, as they went,
Each such power as Fate had lent;
Which, if it united were,
Wretched mortals could not bear.   10
But, as parting friends do show
To what place they mean to go,
Correspondence to engage,
Nominate their utmost stage;
Death declare he would be found
Near the fatal trumpet's sound;
Or where pestilences reign,
And quacks the greater plagues maintain;
Shaking still his sandy glass,
And mowing human flesh, like grass.   20
Love, as next his leave he took,
Cast on both so sweet a look,
As their tempers near disarmed,
One relaxed, and t'other warmed;
Shades for his retreat he chose,
Rural plains and soft repose;
Where no dowry e'er was paid,
Where no jointure e'er was made,
No ill tongue the nymph perplexed,
Where no forms the shepherd vexed;   30
Where himself should be the care
Of the fond and of the fair:
Where that was, they soon should know.
Au revoir! then turned to go.

65

Reputation made a pause
Suiting her severer laws;
Second thoughts and third she used,
Weighing consequences mused;
When at length to both she cried:
"You two safely may divide,   40
To the Antipodes may fall
And reascend the encompassed ball;
Certain still to meet agen
In the breasts of tortured men,
Who, by one too far betrayed,
Call in t'other to their aid:
Whilst I, tender, coy, and nice,
Raised and ruined in a trice
Either fix with those I grace,
Or, abandoning the place,   50
No return my nature bears,
From green youth, or hoary hairs;
If through guilt, or chance, I sever,
I, once parting, part for ever."

There's No Tomorrow

a Fable imitated from Sir Roger L'Estrange

Two long had loved, and now the nymph desired
The cloak of wedlock, as the case required;
Urged that the day he wrought her to this sorrow,
He vowed that he would marry her to-morrow.
Again he swears, to shun the present storm,
That he to-morrow will that vow perform.
The morrows in their due succession came;
Impatient still on each, the pregnant dame
Urged him to keep his word, and still he swore the same.

When tired at length, and meaning no redress,   10
But yet the lie not caring to confess,
He for his oath this salvo chose to borrow,
That he was free, since there was no to-morrow:
For when it comes in place to be employed,
'Tis then to-day: to-morrow's ne'er enjoyed!
The tale's a jest, the moral is a truth:
To-morrow and to-morrow cheat our youth.
    In riper age, to-morrow still we cry,
Not thinking that the present day we die,
Unpractised all the good we had designed: 20
There's no to-morrow to a willing mind.

To the Nightingale

Exert thy voice, sweet harbinger of spring!
    This moment is thy time to sing,
    This moment I attend to praise
And set my numbers to thy lays.
    Free as thine shall be my song,
    As thy music, short or long.
Poets wild as thou were born
    Pleasing best when unconfined,
    When to please is least designed,
Soothing but their cares to rest.   10
    Cares do still their thoughts molest,
    And still the unhappy poet's breast,
Like thine, when best he sings, is placed against a thorn.

She begins. Let all be still!
    Muse, thy promise now fulfil!
Sweet, oh sweet, still sweeter yet!
Can thy words such accents fit,
Canst thou syllables refine,

67

Melt a sense that shall retain
Still some spirit of the brain,   20
Till with sounds like these it join?
   'Twill not be! then change thy note;
   Let division shake thy throat.
Hark! Division now she tries;
Yet as far the Muse outflies.
   Cease then, prithee, cease thy tune.
   Trifler, wilt thou sing till June?
Till thy business all lies waste,
And the time of building's past!
   Thus we poets that have speech,   30
Unlike what thy forests teach,
   If a fluent vein be shown
   That's transcendent to our own,
Criticise, reform, or preach,
Or censure what we cannot reach.

The Dog and his Master

No better dog e'er kept his master's door
Than honest Snarl, who spared not rich nor poor,
But gave the alarm when anyone drew nigh,
Not let pretended friends pass fearless by:
For which reproved, as better fed than taught,
He rightly thus expostulates the fault.

   To keep the house from rascals was my charge:
The task was great, and the commission large.
Nor did your worship e'er declare your mind
That to the begging crew it was confined,   10
Who shrink an arm, or prop an able knee,
Or turn up eyes till they're not seen, nor see;
To thieves who know the penalty of stealth

And fairly stake their necks against your wealth;
These are the known delinquents of the times,
And whips and Tyburn testify their crimes:
But since to me there was by nature lent
An exquisite discerning by the scent,
I trace a flatt'rer when he fawns and leers,
A rallying wit when he commends and jeers;   20
The greedy parasite I grudging note,
Who praises the good bits that oil his throat.
I mark the lady you so fondly toast,
Who plays your gold, when all her own is lost;
The knave who fences your estate by law,
Yet still reserves an undermining flaw.
These and a thousand more, which I could tell,
Provoke my growling and offend my smell.

The Atheist and the Acorn

"Methinks this world is oddly made,
    And everything's amiss,"
A dull presuming atheist said,
As stretched he lay beneath a shade,
    And instanced in this:

"Behold," quoth he, "that mighty thing,
    A pumpkin, large and round,
Is held but by a little string,
Which upwards cannot make it spring,
    Or bear it from the ground;

"Whilst on this oak, a fruit so small,
    So disproportioned, grows;
That, who with sense surveys this All,
This universal casual ball,
    Its ill contrivance knows.

"My better judgment would have hung
    That weight upon a tree,
And left this mast, thus slightly strung,
'Mongst things which on the surface sprung,
    And small and feeble be."

No more the caviller could say,
    Nor farther faults descry;
For, as he upwards gazing lay,
An acorn loosened from the stay
    Fell down upon his eye.

The offended part with tears ran o'er,
    As punished for the sin;
Fool! had that bough a pumpkin bore,
Thy whimsies must have worked no more,
    Nor skull had kept them in.

A Nocturnal Reverie

In such a night, when every louder wind
Is to its distant cavern safe confined;
And only gentle zephyr fans his wings,
And lonely Philomel, still waking, sings;
Or from some tree, famed for the owl's delight,
She, hollowing clear, directs the wanderer right;
In such a night, when passing clouds give place,
Or thinly veil the heaven's mysterious face;

When in some river, overhung with green,
The waving moon and trembling leaves are seen; 10
When freshened grass now bears itself upright,
And makes cool banks to pleasing rest invite,
Whence springs the woodbine and the bramble-rose,
And where the sleepy cowslip sheltered grows;
Whilst now a paler hue the foxglove takes,
Yet chequers still with red the dusky brakes:
When scattered glow-worms, but in twilight fine,
Show trivial beauties watch their hour to shine;
When odours, which declined repelling day,
Through temperate air uninterrupted stray; 20
When darkened groves their softest shadows wear,
And falling waters we distinctly hear;
When through the gloom more venerable shows
Some ancient fabric, awful in repose,
While sunburnt hills their swarthy looks conceal,
And swelling haycocks thicken up the vale:
When the loosed horse now, as his pasture leads,
Comes slowly grazing through the adjoining meads,
Whose stealing pace, and lengthened shade we fear,
Till torn-up forage in his teeth we hear: 30
When nibbling sheep at large pursue their food,
And unmolested kine rechew the cud;
When curlews cry beneath the village walls,
And to her straggling brood the partridge calls;
Their short-lived jubilee the creatures keep,
Which but endures while tyrant man does sleep:
When a sedate content the spirit feels,
And no fierce light disturbs, whilst it reveals;
But silent musings urge the mind to seek
Something, too high for syllables to speak; 40
Till the free soul to a composedness charmed,
Finding the elements of rage disarmed,
O'er all below a solemn quiet grown,
Joys in the inferior world, and thinks it like her own:

In such a night let me abroad remain,
Till morning breaks, and all's confused again;
Our cares, our toils, our clamours are renewed,
Or pleasures, seldom reached, pursued.

To a Fellow Scribbler

Prithee, friend, that hedge behold:
When all we rhyming fools grow old,
That hedge our state will represent,
Who in vain flourish life have spent:
Amidst it stands a rivalled tree
Now representing sixty-three,
And like it you and I shall be.
The bare vine round about it clings
With mischievous, entangling strings,
The night-shade with a dismal flower,   10
Curls o'er it, like a lady's tower;
Or honesty with feathered down,
Like grizzled hair deforms its crown;
Luxuriant plants that o'er it spread,
Not med'cinal for heart or head,
Which serve but to amuse the sight,
Are like the nothings that we write.
Yet still 'tis thought that tree's well placed,
With beauteous eglantine embraced:
But see how false appearance proves,   20
If he that honeysuckle loves;
His love the honeysuckle scorns,
Which climbs by him to reach the thorns;
The rival thorn his age derides,
And gnaws like jealousy his sides.
Then let us cease, my friend, to sing
When ever youth is on the wing,

Unless we solidly indite,
Some good infusing while we write;
Lest with our follies hung around,   30
We like that tree and hedge be found,
Grotesque and trivial, shunned by all,
And soon forgotten when we fall.

The Fall of Caesar

When Caesar fell, he braved each killing wound,
And awful lay dictator on the ground.
But when a friend, or something nearer thought,
Imposed a stab, who should relief have brought;
The dying hero hid his generous face,
When blushes rose in scorn of human race.

Mary Magdalen at Our Saviour's Tomb
a Fragment

'Twas scarce the dawn, nor yet the distant east
Of night's dark shades was dispossessed,
Scarce to the verge approached the rising day,
When weeping Mary to the tomb
Where her dear Redeemer lay
Brings her second rich perfume,
Does new floods of tears prepare,
Once more dedicates her hair,
Which his feet had bathed and dried,
Now to bind His hands and side;
Cruel spear! to close that wound
Where thy steel a passage found,
When thy senseless bearer ran
On the seeming vanquished man.

To the Revd Mr Bedford

On me then Sir, as on a friend,
You say your interests now depend;
And may you be no longer mine
When your least service I decline.
But though my will is all on fire
To compass that which you desire,
Success from others must proceed;
Towards which observe my restless speed.
Your note received, down stairs I fly,
My gown unpinned, my hood awry,   10
With Mrs Mary at my heels.
Who as she this disaster feels,
Here gives a twitch, there aims a pin,
But cannot reach to fix it in –
Yet does with lengthened strides approach
And throws my ruffles in the coach,
I finishing as best I can.
Now draw my gloves and then my fan,
As Jehu scours along the streets
And swears at every thing he meets,   20
Till to his Lordship's door he comes;
Who spies me through a suite of rooms,
And forward moves with courtly pace –
Till, noting my requesting face,
He puts on a refusing air
And bids his footman call a chair.
Then draws his watch – 'tis two and past,
"You find me in prodigious haste,"
He cries as he on tiptoe stands,
"Yet, Madam, what are your commands?   30
I'll serve you to my utmost power –
The Houses have been met this hour –
Shall I conduct you to my wife?
I have no interest, on my life.

I'm ruined if I come too late –
We're like to have a warm debate –
I promised Solon to attend."
"'Tis he, my lord, must help my friend,"
I barely hint as he goes on;
Who, "Madam," cries, "it can't be done. 40
Your humble servant you forgive –
You see in what a round we live,
From morning hurried thus till night.
Madam, I hope you take me right.
When I've a moment to dispose,
I'll come and hear what you propose.
Make haste, you blockheads!" – Up they weigh
My lord, and to the House convey.
Whilst in the parlour I remain,
O'ercome with sorrow and disdain. 50
Yet with a Roman virtue scorn
The Lord depraved where I was born
Where men, now wealthy grown and great,
En bagatelle our suffering treat –
Yet still I will your cause pursue.
The unrighteous judge, the hardened Jew
As soon might be at rest as I
Will leave them till they all comply
Or if no good from thence I draw
They still are Jews without the law. 60

The Agreeable

She is not fair, you critics of the town
That court her smiles and tremble at her frown,
She is not fair, and though I burn like you,
I to my better judgment will be true;
Nor could a painter borrow from her face

75

One line that might his fancied Venus grace;
No feature that might countenance the rest
Is perfect or superlative confest;
Whence then without a charm that we can tell
Does all that's charming in Valeria dwell?
What is the agreeable with which she kills,
And wanting all, all Beauty's part fulfils?
That whensoe'er she speaks, or looks, or moves,
The observer listens, sighs, admires, and loves,
And wonders at the unexpected smart,
Who sees no quiver though he feels the dart?
What is this power which we can ne'er descry,
That nicely shuns not an ill-coloured eye
Nor does from disproportion fly?
What is this charm but something from the soul
Which warms us whilst it shines, and influences the whole;
That mocks description, which can ne'er advance
Their all-subduing mind dressed à la negligence.

A Ballad to Mrs Catherine Fleming in London from Malshanger Farm in Hampshire

From me, who whilom sung the town,
    This second ballad comes,
To let you know we are got down
    From hurry, smoke, and drums,
And every visitor that rowls
In restless coach from Mall to Paul's,
    With a fa-la-la-la-la-la.

And now were I to paint the seat,
    (As well-bred poets use;)
I should embellish our retreat,

10

By favour of the muse:
Tho' to no villa we pretend,
But a plain farm at the best end.
   With a fa-la &c.

Where innocence and quiet reigns,
   And no distrust is known;
His nightly safety none maintains,
   By ways they do in Town:
Who rising loosen bolt and bar,
We draw the latch and out we are.   20
   With a fa-la &c.

For jarring sounds in London streets,
   Which still are passing by;
Where "Cowcumbers" with "Sand ho" meets,
   And for loud mastery vie:
The driver whistling to his team,
Here wakes us from some rural dream.
   With a fa-la &c.

From rising hills thro' distant views,
   We see the Sun decline;   30
Whilst every where the eye pursues,
   The grazing flocks and kine:
Which home at night the farmer brings,
And not the post's but sheep's bell rings
   With a fa-la &c.

We silver trouts and cray-fish eat,
   Just taken from the stream;
And never think our meal compleat,
   Without fresh curds and cream:
And as we pass by the barn floor,   40
We choose our supper from the door.
   With a fa-la &c.

Beneath our feet the partridge springs,
    As to the woods we go;
Where birds scarce stretch their painted wings,
    So little fear they shew:
But when our outspread hoops they spy,
They look when we like them should fly.
    With a fa-la &c.

Thro' verdant circles as we stray,   50
    To which no end we know;
As we o'er hanging boughs survey,
    And tufted grass below:
Delight into the fancy falls,
And happy days and verse recalls.
    With a fa-la &c.

Oh! why did I these shades forsake,
    And shelter of the grove;
The flowring shrub the rustling brake,
    The solitude I love: 60
Where emperors have fixed their lot,
And greatly chose to be forgot.
    With a fa-la &c.

Then how can I from hence depart,
    Unless my pleasing friend;
Should now her sweet harmonious art,
    Unto these shades extend:
And like old Orpheus' powerful song,
Draw me and all my woods along.
    With a fa-la &c.   70

So charmed like Birnam's they would rise,
    And march in goodly row,
But since it might the town surprise,
    To see me travel so:

I must from soothing joys like these,
Too soon return in open chaise:
    With a fa-la &c.

Mean while accept what I have writ,
    To shew this rural scene;
Nor look for sharp satyric wit,   80
    From off the balmy plain:
The country breeds no thorny bays,
    But mirth and love and honest praise.
    With a fa-la &c.

Sir Plausible

Sir Plausible, as 'tis well known,
Has no opinions of his own;
But closes with each stander by,
Now in a truth, now in a lie,
Fast as chameleons change their dye;
Has still some applicable story
To gratify a Whig or Tory,
And even a Jacobite in tatters
If met alone he smoothly flatters;
Greets friend and foe with wishes fervent,
And lives and dies your humble servant.

A Song on the South Sea, 1720

Ombre and basset laid aside,
  New games employ the fair;
And brokers all those hours divide
  Which lovers used to share.

The court, the park, the foreign song
  And harlequin's grimace
Forlorn; amidst the city throng
  Behold each blooming face.

With Jews and Gentiles undismayed
  Young tender virgins mix;
Of whiskers nor of beards afraid,
  Nor all the cozening tricks.

Bright jewels, polished once to deck
  The fair one's rising breast,
Or sparkle round her ivory neck,
  Lie pawned in iron chest.

The gayer passions of the mind
  How avarice controls!
Even love does now no longer find
  A place in female souls.

Notes

Fragment, p.17
 2   *Ardelia*   A.F.'s name for herself
 14   *the wheel*   i.e. of fortune
 23   Wye College in Kent was formerly a priory

The Bird, p.18
 14   *Phoebus*   Greek god of the sun

A Letter to Daphnis, p.20
     Daphnis   A.F.'s name for her husband

The Tree, p.21
 12   *reed*   rustic musical instrument made from the hollow
     stem of a plant

To Mr F., now Earl of Winchilsea, p.23
 7   *Parnassus*   a mountain in Greece, sacred to the muses
 31   *sisters*   the four muses mentioned in the poem
 43   *Erato*   the muse of love poetry
     Grizel   the medieval type of long-suffering wife – see
     the *Decameron* and Chaucer's "Clerk's Tale"
 44   *Troy Town*   see *The Iliad*
     Chevy Chase   one of the oldest English ballads, dating
     from the fourteenth century
 61   *Pegasus*   the winged horse, on which poets took their
     flights of fancy, was overworked with poems in praise
     of William
 67   *Melpomene*   muse of comedy
 70   *Thalia*   muse of tragedy
 73   *Urania*   muse of heavenly love
 92   *Hymen*   god of marriage

The Introduction, p.26
 25-36   A.F. here cites from Jewish history three examples of
     women poets. See in the Old Testament: I Chronicles 15;
     I Samuel 18; Judges 4,5

The Ark was an acacia chest, the holiest object of Jewish religious furniture.

To a Friend, p.29
28   See Genesis 41,42

To my Sister Ogle, p.30
Dorothy Ogle was A.F.'s half-sister, the only child of her mother's remarriage
13   See Joshua 10: 12,13 for the lengthening of the day to enable Joshua to finish off his enemies.

The Change, p.31
Myra Reynolds read the poem as an "allegory of the selfishness and insincerity of courtiers," with the sun, the river and the mansion as "pictures of the discrowned king."

An Invitation to Daphnis, p.38
25   *Sanson's World*   a French geography published in 1700
31 ff.   A.F. is referring to the war against Louis XIV of France
Vauban   the French military engineer
Orpheus's lyre-playing enabled him to make animals, trees and rocks follow him
59   *Baucis and Philemon*   the legendary model of a married couple. They died in the same hour and were turned into trees

The Spleen, p.40
2   *Proteus*   a prophetic old man who was able to change his shape to avoid capture
20   *Brutus*   a leading conspirator in the assassination of Julius Caesar in 44 B.C. In the subsequent civil war he was defeated by Octavian at the battle of Philippi, and took his own life.
88   See the story of Balaam and the ass in the Old Testament, Numbers 22: 21-35
141   *Lower*   a well-known London surgeon, the first to transfuse blood from one animal to another.

Ardelia's Answer to Ephelia, p.45

Ephelia cannot be identified

74 *Dryden* the poet and dramatist, 1631-1700. Sir George Etherege and Nathaniel Lee were dramatists of the second half of the seventeenth century

82 The craze for the best in imported china meant that customers boarded the ships before they had unloaded their cargo of tea

150 *Adonis* a beautiful youth loved by Aphrodite (whose Roman name was Venus)

153 *Venus* sprang from the foam of the sea near Cythera, an island in the Mediterranean

157 *Piso* Lord Roscommon produced a translation of Horace's *Ars Poetica* and an essay on "Translated Verse"

159 *Silenus* In Greek mythology a fat old man depicted as drunk and garlanded with flowers

207 On Mount Helicon in the Peloponnese there was a temple sacred to the muses

The Petition for an Absolute Retreat, p.53

31 *ortolan* a small wild bird considered a delicacy

36-48 These lines echo Marvell's "The Garden", "What wondrous life is this I lead! / Ripe apples drop about my head . . ."

59 *monarch* Solomon

77 See Genesis 26

93 *Lucullus* Roman politician who after some successful campaigning in the East returned to Rome and devoted the rest of his life (to 56 B.C.) to luxurious living

182 *son of Jess* David. See Samuel 16-30

206 *Crassus* A wealthy but ineffectual Roman politician, who was assassinated in 53 B.C. A.F.'s account comes from Plutarch's *Life of Crassus*, according to her own note.

253 The Canary Islands were once known as the Fortunate Islands

Jupiter and the Farmer, p.64

Zeus (Roman name Jupiter), the more or less supreme god of the Greeks, was brought up in a cave in Crete. Shut up in a tower to prevent her having a child, Danaë was visited by Zeus in the form of a shower of gold and bore a son, Perseus

6   *Mercury*   the Roman god of traders

To the Nightingale, p.67

division   i.e. of a series of long notes into a series of short ones

The Dog and his Master, p.68

16   *Tyburn*   a part of London used for public executions

A Nocturnal Reverie, p.70

4   *Philomel*   daughter of a King of Athens was turned into a nightingale after she had been seduced by Tereus

To a Fellow Scribbler, p.72

10   Woody nightshade
12   *honesty*   wild clematis, known nowadays as traveller's joy or old man's beard

The Fall of Caesar, p.73

3   *a friend*   i.e. Brutus; see note on "The Spleen", line 20

A Fragment on Mary Magdalen at the Tomb, p.73

See Mark 16 or John 20

To the Revd Mr Bedford, p.74

Bedford was a non-juror clergyman who hoped for the help of a peer to advance his interests

19   *Jehu*   a fast driver; see II Kings 9: 20
26   *chair*   a sedan chair
32   *Houses*   i.e. of Parliament, the Lords and the Commons
34   *interest*   influence
37   *Solon*   the Athenian law-giver who flourished about 600 B.C.

54   *en bagatelle*   as a trifle

A Ballad to Mrs Catherine Fleming, p.76
    24   Street cries by sellers of cucumbers and sand used for
          cleaning
    68   *Orpheus*   see note on "An Invitation to Daphnis", line 31
    71   *Birnam's*   in Shakespeare's play Macbeth was assured by
          witches that he would be safe till Birnam wood came to
          Dunsinane

Sir Plausible, p.79
    8   *Jacobite*   a supporter of the Stuart cause after the abdication
          of James II

A Song on the South Sea, p.80
          The South Sea Bubble (1711-1720) was a speculative scheme
          for exploiting the South Sea trade; it ruined thousands of
          investors

Books Consulted

Sources

The Spleen, A Pindarique Ode by a lady
Together with J. Pomfret's *A Prospect of Death A Pindarique Essay*
London, 1709
Miscellany Poems on Several Occasions Written by a Lady London,
1713
Manuscript at Wellesley College, Massachusetts, contains poems
written after 1713

Editions and Selections

The Poems of Anne, Countess of Winchilsea, edited by Myra Reynolds
Chicago, 1903. Includes all the poems accessible in 1903, with a
full introduction that is especially valuable for biographical
material and its account of Anne Finch's reputation in the nine-
teenth century
Poems and Extracts chosen by William Wordsworth for an album
presented to Lady Mary Lowther, Christmas, 1819, published by
Henry Frowde, 1905. Contains thirty-two Anne Finch poems
Selected Poems of Anne, Countess of Winchilsea Orinda Booklets,
Hull, 1906
Poems by Anne, Countess of Winchilsea Selected and with an
Introductory Essay by John Middleton Murry London, 1928
Minor Poets of the Eighteenth Century, edited by H. I'A. Fausset,
Everyman's Library, 1930. Contains 116 pages of Anne Finch
poems, and is mainly a reprint of the 1713 volume
Pope's Own Miscellany (a reprint of *Poems on Several Occasions* 1717)
edited by Norman Ault, Nonesuch Press, 1935
Selected Poems of Anne Finch, edited by Katharine M. Rogers
Frederick Ungar, New York, c.1979
The World Split Open, Women Poets 1552-1950, edited by Louise
Bernikow The Women's Press, 1979

Criticism

W. Wordsworth	Essay, Supplementary to the Preface to the second edition of the *Lyrical Ballads*
	Letters to Alexander Dyce, 16 October 1829, 5 May 1830
Leigh Hunt	*The Companion*, May-July, 1828
Edmund Gosse	*Gossip in a Library*, 1891
Edward Dowden	*Essays, Modern and Elizabethan*, 1910
Helen Sard Hughes	*London Mercury*, Vol. XIX, pp. 624 ff.
Middleton Murry	*Countries of the Mind*, Second series, Oxford, 1931
W.H. Williams ed.	*The Spleen, by Matthew Green*, London, 1936
H.N. Fairchild	*Religious Trends in English Poetry*, Vol. 1, Columbia University Press, 1936
R.A. Brower	"Lady Winchilsea and the Poetic Tradition of the Seventeenth Century", *Studies in Philology*, Vol. 42, pp. 61 ff.
Norman Callan	*Pelican Guide to English Literature*, Vol. 4, pp. 357-362, 1957
S.M. Gilbert and Susan Gubar ed.	*Shakespeare's Sisters*, article by Katharine Rogers, pp. 37-46, 1979
W.J. Cameron	*Anne, Countess of Winchilsea: a Guide for the Future Biographer* (thesis, Victoria University of Wellington, New Zealand)

Index of First Lines

"The Fyfield Books series provides an admirable service in publishing good inexpensive selections from the works of interesting but neglected poets"
– *British Book News*

THOMAS LOVELL BEDDOES (1803-49)
Selected Poems
edited by Judith Higgens

THE BRONTË SISTERS
Selected Poems
edited by Stevie Davies

ELIZABETH BARRETT BROWNING (1806-61)
Selected Poems
edited by Malcolm Hicks

THOMAS CAMPION (1567-1620)
Ayres and Observations
edited by Joan Hart

GEORGE CHAPMAN (?1559-1634)
Selected Poems
edited by Eirean Wain

THOMAS CHATTERTON (1752-70)
Selected Poems
edited by Grevel Lindop

CHARLES COTTON (1630-87)
Selected Poems
edited by Ken Robinson

WILLIAM COWPER (1731-1800)
Selected Poems
edited by Nick Rhodes

GEORGE CRABBE (1754-1832)
Selected Poems
edited by Jem Poster

RICHARD CRASHAW (1612/13-49)
Selected Poems
edited by Michael Cayley

MICHAEL DRAYTON (1563-1631)
Selected Poems
edited by Vivian Thomas

GEORGE GASCOIGNE (1530-77)
The Green Knight:
selected poems and prose
edited by Roger Pooley

JOHN GAY (1685-1732)
Selected Poems
edited by Marcus Walsh

JOHN GOWER (1330-1408)
Selected Poetry
edited by Carole Weinberg

THOMAS GRAY (1716-71)
Selected Poems
edited by John Heath-Stubbs

ROBERT HENRYSON (1425?-1508?)
Selected Poems
edited by W.R.J. Barron

ROBERT HERRICK (1591-1674)
Selected Poems
edited by David Jesson-Dibley

THOMAS HOCCLEVE (?1348-1430)
Selected Poems
edited by Bernard O'Donoghue

BEN JONSON (1572-1637)
Epigrams & The Forest
edited by Richard Dutton

WALTER SAVAGE LANDOR (1775-1864)
Selected Poems and Prose
edited by Keith Hanley

ANDREW MARVELL (1621-78)
Selected Poems
edited by Bill Hutchings

GEORGE MEREDITH (1828-1909)
Selected Poems
edited by Keith Hanley

CHARLES OF ORLEANS (1394-1465)
Selected Poems
edited by Sally Purcell

SIR WALTER RALEGH (?1554-1618)
Selected Writings
edited by Gerald Hammond

JOHN WILMOT, EARL OF ROCHESTER
(1648-80)
The Debt to Pleasure
edited by John Adlard

CHRISTINA ROSSETTI (1830-94)
Selected Poems
edited by C.H. Sisson

SIR PHILIP SIDNEY (1554-86)
Selected Poetry and Prose
edited by Richard Dutton

JOHN SKELTON (1460-1529)
Selected Poems
edited by Gerald Hammond

CHRISTOPHER SMART (1722-71)
Selected Poems
edited by Marcus Walsh

DONALD STANFORD (editor)
Three Poets of the Rhymers' Club:
Lionel Johnson, Ernest Dowson,
John Davidson

HENRY HOWARD, EARL OF SURREY
(1517-47)
Selected Poems
edited by Dennis Keene

JONATHAN SWIFT (1667-1745)
Selected Poems
edited by C.H. Sisson

ALGERNON CHARLES SWINBURNE
(1837-1909)
Selected Poems
edited by L.M. Findlay

ARTHUR SYMONS (1865-1945)
Selected Writings
edited by R.V. Holdsworth

THOMAS TRAHERNE (?1637-74)
Selected Writings
edited by Dick Davis

HENRY VAUGHAN (1622-95)
Selected Poems
edited by Robert B. Shaw

ANNE FINCH, COUNTESS OF WINCHILSEA
(1661-1720)
Selected Poems
edited by Denys Thompson

EDWARD YOUNG (1683-1765)
Selected Poems
edited by Brian Hepworth

"Carcanet are doing an excellent job in this series: the editions are labours of love, not just commercial enterprises. I hope they are familiar to all readers and teachers of literature." – *Times Literary Supplement*